This is Love

This is Love
Poetry & Prose

Carolyn Riker

GOLDEN DRAGONFLY PRESS
Amherst, Massachusetts
2018

FIRST PRINT EDITION, June 2018
FIRST EBOOK EDITION, June 2018

Front cover art by Debby Hudson.
Copyright © 2018 by Carolyn Riker (Carolyn Avalani).

First published in the United States of America
by Golden Dragonfly Press, 2018.

ISBN-13: 978–0–9989766–7–9
ISBN-10: 0–9989766–7–9

Library of Congress Control Number: 2018942114

www.goldendragonflypress.com

CONTENTS

Introduction   xi

SECTION I
Self-Love

To Be Loved   5

Complete Self   6

Eye of Soul   7

Kiss of Autumn   8

I Love You   9

A Need to Drift   10

I Am a Note   11

Prism Inside of a Storm   12

Alone   14

Quiet   15

Kindness is Divine   16

A Love Affair with Coffee   17

The Mirror   18

Solo Isn't a Tragedy   19

Love is a Paradigm   20

Courage   21

Go Gently   22

Blueprint of Soul   23

Just Listen   24

Daydream   25

We Hear the Remembering   26

The Beginning of Me   27

I'm Not a Number on a Scale   29

Self-Acceptance   30

Curves of My Soul   31

Empty Isn't Love   33

Your Soul's Holy   34

The Paradox of Poetry   35

She Sang the Blues   36

All the Sides of Me   37

You'd be Dead if You Didn't Feel   38

Heart-Path   39

Soul's Thoughts   40

Love Writes Me   41

You Matter   43

To Be Loved   44

SECTION II
Love Is

Earth is a Dance   47

Wildest Blooms   48

Discovery   49

Love's Joys   50

Rose Soaked Rhapsody   51

Soft, Gentle, Soft   52

The Art of Tea   53

Hearts   55

Summoned by Moonlight   56

Square Root of Nothingness   57

A Circle of Holy   58

Grief's Love   59

Imagination   60

Love is   61

Tired 63

Deeply Felt 64

Joni Mitchell Like 66

Out There 68

Colors Under My Skin 70

Circles 71

What is Love? 72

Joying is Living 73

When Love is Real 74

Silence Becomes the Words 76

Our Dreaming Song 77

Thanking Love 78

L–O–V–E 81

Being Loved 83

Home 84

SECTION III
Relationships
What Love is and isn't

Goodbyes Have Full Memories 87

Letting Go 88

Let's Be Flight's Love 89

What Isn't Said 90

To Love Again 91

Respect 92

Friendship 93

You Didn't Notice 94

Wholeness Needs Support 95

Letting Go, Isn't Easy 96

Stained-Glass Wings 98

Boundaries   99
Nothing is Forever   100
Ordinary is Extraordinary   101
I Am Not You   102
No Longer Chasing You   104
Unspoken   106
You   107
Just a Lifetime   108
No Perfect Needed   109
Words Can Bite   110
Just a Note   111
Pain   112
Tongue-Tied   113
Because of You   114
Just Dance   116
By the River   117
I Tried   119
Push-Pull Me Wrong   120
I noticed   121
Thank You   122
Stop It   123
Last Poem I Wrote for You   124
Speak Real   125
Again   126
Insights   127
For What Isn't   128
Love is Never Far   129
Sit with Me   131
Parchment of Our Soul   132
When We Meet   134
About the Author   137

This book is dedicated to my close friends, teachers and mentors who have taught me about love by loving me in my steady imperfections. It is for Kyle and Genevieve and Copper because you are love. If you know me, even a little, you are a part of this dream because much of what I write is inspired by my connections—I warmly thank you all.

INTRODUCTION

*O*ne of my favorite things to do is to write, especially in small coffee shops like where I happen to be right now. *This is Love*, is a collection of poetry and prose that I've been writing for a few years. Pieces came through in difficult times and others in lighter. My sensitivity is poetry.

Sticky notes and notepads clutter nearly every flat space around me because I never know when colors will trip over tongue and I'll need to taste the words streaming through. Frequently I feel like a conduit and intertwined between this world and somewhere else.

Inspiration to write isn't always pleasant. Just when I amusingly think–*oh, that doesn't hurt me anymore; I'm over jealousy, sadness, divorce, anger, fear, loneliness. I get what love is.* Pop! There goes that illusion. Bubbles splatter everywhere. I'm a mess and I'm faced with a whole new learning usually ambushed by my own unconscious complexes revealed by what someone says or does, and the trigger of what love is or isn't leaks, speaks and tumbles over love's rocky shores. Poetry is birthed.

Love comes in a myriad of disguises. Thankfully it's here to teach us. I find the stronger emotions are some of the most passionate as motivating guides that bring poetry to fruition.

While selecting pieces for this book, three sections seemed to fall kindly into place and all over my living room floor. My round ginger cat, Copper lovingly supervised in his pancake-like form.

This is Love holds a spot about self-love, as well as love is everywhere and finally the highs and lows of love and relationships. I struggled the most with sections one and three because I'm still learning about self-love and relationships. The middle part represents nature and things that ground me. If all-parts-equal-a-whole theory is true–then thank goodness because I'm slowly getting there.

Simply put, love is everything and not. Love hurts, cries and joys. Love finds hope. Love celebrates. Love ends and begins. Love is respect. Love isn't an exact science. Sometimes, I wish it were easier, but it isn't. Love finds us in our darkest nights as well as our darkest days. Love is justice.

Right now, I'm that woman in the corner of a coffee shop all teary writing this because if you are holding this book and reading these words, I know you and I will be meeting and seeing *This is Love* inside of my heart.

With love & hugs,
Carolyn

SECTION I

Self-Love

I will trace
each word born;
until the mysteries
inside of me
become its
colors.

TO BE LOVED

"Every secret of a writer's soul, every experience of her life, every quality of her mind, is written large in her words."

—Virginia Woolf

The experiences in our lifetime hopefully teach us; oftentimes favorably and other times, not. It is between these two states we untangle inconsistencies wedged in peace and chaos. If we are fortunate we take what we have learned and fold it inside out. We look at what isn't to see what is. We look for truths. When I experience an edge of one of these truths, I soar, crumble and dissolve into it all. Each time I write I share another layer of me and another segment of me gets stronger.

To feel loved, to be loved, and to give love is a transparent offering. To be seen and heard is without a doubt remarkable. To listen and hear, priceless. When we love, we show it. We find words and ways. We set aside time. It's not a chore. We don't try to destroy or change the person into someone else. We let them be themselves. We don't stop their growth; instead we rejoice in their growth.

To be loved we are accepted for who we are. Vulnerability is poignant. Raw is real. To be loved and to love, takes courage; to be fully seen is incredibly rare and breathtaking. We lower our masks and see a celestial inner being; it is the whole of our self—the supernova as well as the black holes. Our fears and doubts. Our anger and joy. We witness the expansion and the unknowing parts of our self in this space of safety. This is love.

COMPLETE SELF

We learn to be our complete self as we stand strong in our self-acceptance. Not letting others diminish who we are. Each of us has something to offer, share and do. It's our superpowers. No one can ever take that away from me or you.

EYE OF SOUL

I became the petals
the softness of love
I wedded the thorns of death
and birthed the buds of new.
I became the eye of soul
and caressed the wilted.
I was the defeated cries
and tender mercy of redemption.
I returned the seeds of hopes
and became a flower with
renewed will.

KISS OF AUTUMN

Flannel feels
and the day
unfolds me messy
into pillowed dreams
crisp air,
dazes
dense greens,
tinged
with kiss of autumn
breath slows
eyes wane closed
dozing soft and silent
as rain dances
on still waters
as flannel feels
hold my hands
with prose.

I Love You

I saw you in my dream. Small, fragile and tender. I saw you shivering, shaking, soulfully transparent. I just knew, in that magical misty moment, I had to hold you and let you know, I love you.

A Need to Drift

Please understand
when I drift and drift
away from all of this
and that and those things
that get tangled behind
my eye thoughts; all my heart
doesn't fit in this world.
My skin starts to crawl. So please
understand, I need to drift and
drift until I find midnight's
peaceful whale song.

I Am a Note

I am a poem
where my wistful
is weathered by clouded light
and scars are but fallen stars.

I am a hollow circle
of fruited wood trees
plucked chords ring
over blazed sun
knitted kin to comet.

I am rinsed in the thoughts
of slanted raindrops;
wind becomes shield
to my soul's shivered branches.

I am a note scribed sleepless
captured in hell or rapture;
for each word is a process
to retrieve the unfinished
poems of heart.

PRISM INSIDE OF A STORM

She thought, "I don't belong here." But the rain pulled her clear.

You are sometimes a mirage in a rainstorm. You don't exactly fit the proper, the protocol and therefore, have every right to disappear. Words, like music, are emotions and colors that need porcelain precision to process; to be painted and twisted into an aperture to see-feel. Like creativity, it enlightens and frightens but it lets you breathe into the light and hears through the dark.

You are a prism inside of a storm.

I don't have to
see the stars
to know
they are there.
I just feel them.

ALONE

In the creases of never there's always a tomorrow. Alone can happen in a full room. Some can't relate to the sound of silence. Others have grown callouses around heart. And a handful have the penchant to see there are shades of bittersweet even in the dismal shadows. It is where I find answers that break and bleed blue. Where we separate the self-doubt from the noise of the norm. Knowing what's up also carries the weight of what's down. It gives me golden pearls and slices of wisdom's truths.

QUIET

Sometimes,
the essence of my dreams
are so simple:
the quietness of wings.
And I go there
for miles and miles.

KINDNESS IS DIVINE

I turned light as feather
hallowed wings of holy
tree branches,
a celestial map intertwined
the avenues of life
laid dizzy before me and
stardust held my eyes
little mattered but breath and love
spirals of peace brushed serendipitously
hand over heart, the cold of morning
the silence of seeing,
the fondness of hearing
the colors of feeling
the cresting waves of believing
kindness is divine
love is compassion and
unity is my heart's desire.

A LOVE AFFAIR WITH COFFEE

"I love you." I spoke to my coffee and all hell broke loose. A string of words came tumbling out, making little sense (because nonsense is sometimes needed). I'm a gatherer of non-fancy-things. Pompous annoys me. I prefer to watch and be with autumn trees; they invite me to sing louder. I'm intoxicated by their assortment and cacophony.

Don't try to Photoshop me into a fine art field of elite-isms coveted as, *'you'll look better, wearing that little-black-dress to be seen-with-me.'* It leaves me weary and cuts me. Instead I'll sit and chat with the pixels of people passing through because I'm much happier with the uglier sides of metamorphosis—where my undies fall, and my socks don't match and obviously I have a love affair with coffee.

I don't have the latest and greatest. Sleep is foreign, and reading is equivalent to watering plants. I must expose my really-weird-isms by breathing with leafy freedom of dying yellow, crimson, and burgundy leaves of autumn. What a grand way to learn: behaving unruly by shaking the ground with a calico sound–is also me! (The leaves are clapping!)

Writing this finds me a bit dizzy (and nervous and shy; damn there's so many sides of me) but thankfully evergreens have an unyielding love of emerald glow, and mountains have a top hat of snow forever reminding me: I (we, you, me) don't need to pose and postulate for anyone, anymore. It kinda makes me smile—just being me. And seeing you—just for you—and letting the rest be.

THE MIRROR

If you see me
staring at you
it's because
I'm not sure
who you are.

Those aged lines
grow grey wilder
obscure and shapeless
engulfs ample shores.

Eyes-closed-wide
holds shame inside
dismissing swiftly
the how-to-see
with kinder eyes.

What say you
if we smashed the
scales of lies?
Shoved aside those
mind-word knives?

Maybe then,
minus the world's screen,
the depth inside
can be seen.

Solo Isn't a Tragedy

Skies can be grey or blue or the color of nothingness and no one can take away your dreams. Rain can be silent or angry and still there's a melody. Answers ride on wings of diversity. Joy is felt in laughter and often birthed from ancient seas.

Being solo isn't a tragedy.

What is happening now, most likely will change. Confusion and conflict are the mulch of today and grow into tomorrows. Insights are my yesterdays. I am not less of a person for being without more.

Failures teach, and I will learn and soar.

Twilight sees me, and dawn hears me, but darkness knows me. Forlorn breaches and whale moans surge salinity. That's when creativity is often born.

Madness is not a malady.

Somedays are so still that weeds grow between my toes. Or I can taste the twist of sunshine and trees breathe within me. Unity knits a shawl of silence and love opens to the speed of sound. I treasure the depth of those souls willing to dive deep.

This much I know for sure: Being solo isn't a tragedy.

LOVE IS A PARADIGM

Tiny safe spaces are comfort.
A serenade of bees
Sing the same three notes
'let it be.'

How silence is a waterfall
just before dusk. Stillness
is the inspiration of trees.
Whispers come from evergreens.

How imagination has saved me.
Smiles that close eyes. Knowing
moss meditates. The flavor of lush
is pure and the Blues hum,
more holy than we can see.

Where voices rise in my mind's soul
this is heart. How images
and dreams write me.
When tender-silent
can feel a leaf breathe.
When answers come unexpectedly.
Love is a paradigm finding me.

COURAGE

Show me courage. The creative frenzied tattered boundaries that encircle the underbelly of vulnerable. Our imperfections will take us to the whole of our deeper truths. Let me see-feel into the charcoaled sketch of your real. I want to hear the feral sounds of your predawn fears and the layered dregs of midnight's uncertainties. That place where we can trust in a distrustful world and freed from status quo's relentless disgrace.

Let's declare our heart's visions so we can be clearer and demystify sorrow as wrong, weakness as evil and joy as the only. There's so much more; our diversities are a galaxy of stars beyond stars. Let's unveil the lesser sides we so frequently hide and swell into the colors of sound.

Let's embrace what we already are—limitless and profound as we show the decimals of our exceptional and express the courageous of our deepest self.

Go Gently

One note at a time
swollen together,
dragging each sentiment
through a pinhole's
page of timeless.

Go gently,
chants weary.
Moon's faint curve,
casts a sorcery
on living and dying.

Go slowly,
and breathe the
sounded repeat of
a madrone tree's mantra.

Go softly,
I'll stay with you;
care deeply and
let flight rest in
caverns or precipice.

Go gently,
one note at a time.

Blueprint of Soul

I love seeing people who reach into each other's hearts. I hear laughter and compassion; a deeper space of conversation is being poured. Caring is too often ignored. No one is better than. Each of us can do our part. The differences we have—are a blueprint of our soul. 'Respect' chants a soft foothold. Some will be bold and direct, while others will quietly speak. Everyone is significant in their creativity. Intelligence isn't only about eloquence and status and degrees. The being of a person is what matters.

The diploma of Kindness is more often the tincture needed. And yet? Sometimes we need to be firm and stand clear against the 'isms' inflicting and crippling a minority of souls in this crushing-harsh-world. Therefore, I speak against abuse. I've seen, and experienced violence and trauma more than I wish I had, however something often whispers, "Use that as empathy to hear, feel and see. Don't compare or compete with those who try to restrict you. Write. Create. And be you."

JUST LISTEN

I misplaced my glasses
by the blue flower pot
or maybe not;
perhaps under my chair.

I finally stopped
trying so hard to see
and just listen
to the hyssops
tugging me away
along a full budded tree.

I held on dearly to
to a clover breeze
and saddled up with
a dragon; its allure
incandescently
flung a spell o'er me.

'Till fern's foliage
signaled my venture complete
was I able to see my needs;
a diving quest
to live the edges of fully.

DAYDREAM

If you see me speak unevenly
you know, that pause-thought-stare?
It's because I'm navigating thru
unseen mountainous territory.

Those word-feels need time to bend
from heart to seaworthy. Betrayals
are shaky when gathered together.

How much of life is a river stitching
sunken ash of past? Those daydreams
that craft crazy makeshift paths to stowaway
some of the deepest places we fear to go.

So, if you see me staring thru emptiness,
I'm not lost. I'm finding my way back. And
carrying newly found pieces of me home.

WE HEAR THE REMEMBERING

We need our days, sometimes, to be full of touching quiet and finding song. Music playing in the pine-scented rafters between the sighting of the sun and settling clouds over a seasonal rainy hum. We hear the remembering and need to find a slight cove of resting. Eyes heaving from the accumulating and our senses overflowing—we welcome hours of wandering in the landscape of daydreaming. Awakening to the comforting of split vanilla beans pouring from the heavens. The molasses cookies quiet breathing, we sip warming teas and watching leafing trees become fall. We spend our days, sometimes, full into the heart-hand hoping and rekindling the essence of our being—as we become quieter we hear our inner horizon singing a song.

THE BEGINNING OF ME

I must go now,
just for a while
to regain my footing
from sharp edges.
I'm not spear-proof
and the condensation of
my being is leaking
over slate paths of my solitude;
I'm crumbling into
my own space of softer thoughts
and seeing the end of us,
was the beginning of me.

She looked into the mirror and saw the sea—expansive and wise; the space behind one's eyes. Seeing the center where vision is wild and heard the rules escape on wings of free.

I'm Not a Number on a Scale

For once—it isn't the number
seen on scale, dictating
my fate of win-lose-fail.

Weight, a heaviness
an embodied realness,
fluctuating on wingspan
or swimming with whales.

Self-love is a spiral—inward,
rather than a Fitbit setting of what
society demands. Thinness isn't the
one-and-only.

How top-heavy the bell curve would be
if we all succumbed to such a tyranny?
It's just another controlled setting
to annihilate intelligence's beauty.

Sameness exploits the fears
swarming with perfection;
when truly we are gifted—
imperfectly magnificent.

The flaws, we are not; our hips
and lips and skin color accentuate.
Diversity shouts: "Bleach me no longer
to the confines of ordinary!"

For once, my midyears have redefined.
My body holy-whole is breathing through
silver eyes and dimpled skin and stretch marks
of rivers far and wide. Artificial can
no longer hide.

I am not just a number on a scale.

SELF-ACCEPTANCE

This is a hard one to learn. We want to be accepted by people. We want to belong. We want to be loved. We want to fit in. However, when we chase those who only show up sometimes, or when they feel like it, or give the hot-cold shoulder shrug filtered with double-signals and that wall of "they-are-more-important" and "we-are-lesser." Something is off. This isn't a healthy relationship. There's an imbalance of power, control and rank and we deserve more. We deserve respect for our thoughts, minds, hearts and intelligence. Therefore, I will no longer chase after those who refuse to see my worth.

CURVES OF MY SOUL

And the piano played a melody...
Softly through the nasturtium vines
and into my heart.

In my twenties I searched.
In my thirties I settled down.
In my forties I questioned.
In my fifties I followed my heart.
Aching into the chords, I heard the truth.

Be yourself.

A deep blues mirrored my poetry
and sang to my heartstrings.

You'll be just fine.

The dusty keyboard,
tantalized my fingers
as the music flowed
through the curves of my soul.

I echoed the rhythm.

It rocked my tenderness
and filled the missing keys with love.

Originally published on *elephant journal*, 2015.

"Solitude is the place of purification."
—Martin Buber

We do so much in any given day, even nights become blurry. And before we know it we become battered and bruised from repeated misunderstands. Sometimes, it's hard to translate. Fortunately, twilight received me tonight and angels spoke through moonlit trees: "We all need a bit of self-nurturing."

EMPTY ISN'T LOVE

Morning undid me
to air's chill
quiet's dark
before blues or trills.

Spirits dreamed
worry escaped
alongside doubts
boundaries safe.

No more
buying, vying, needing.
Trusting stopped.
Only a knowing;
empty isn't love.

Your Soul's Holy

I didn't ask to write this—it wrote me. I felt the surge between sunrise and dreams. Footsteps paced in my soul and my arms still not awake, tried to push away the fervor but my fingers ached.

Please write me. Please write the sound of full, the ribbons of hope, and the real of tomorrow. Step into the rise of always. It's a new day; a wake of storms, the silence of sharp and essence of love being explained. You are needed. There's no time to waste.

My sleeves heavy with sleep and uneven stitches, the threads worn elbow to forearm, and I composed into the vein of a cello's soft mourn. I stirred each note with pained ecstasy; it seems to be the bookmark of truth.

Please be you. Find your song. Sing your dance. Love the space and grace of you. Speak loud and soft. Cry the source of rage. Erase the '*shoulds*' and fill with desire. You are needed. The speckled wholeness of diversity is trying to find your soul's holy.

THE PARADOX OF POETRY

Maybe I'm a little lost
when my ribbon's ink has run dry and
my soundness unravels over brook and
voiced wild rivers chase endlessly.

Maybe the moon slips from eye,
fading effortlessly over sky
watching and waiting as, we too,
have our natural decline and rise.

Maybe it's a warning,
as much as charcoal skies end
and seas sharply wither within;
these tempests share me indefinable.

However,
all that I am,
and all that I must,
bravely leads me back
to the paradox of poetry's
medicinal love.

SHE SANG THE BLUES

'Had I known
Had I known
Had I known…'

Was part of the refrain.
Sultry sang it deep blue.

She wore sequins of
midnight and the drummer
brushed a circled sound; keyboard
melted her bones to the bass
of hurt's dark ache.

I don't know if you knew
how much she trusted you.

It chokes her hard when she speaks
So, she sings….

'Had I known
Had I known
Had I known…'

I promise you
she would have never shared
knowing you didn't care.

I told her, be music
until the blues lose hold
and so, she still sings…

I swear,
when I listen
even my heart aches.

ALL THE SIDES OF ME

If all sides of me
were pure and kind
All. Of. The. Time.
It would be so f*cking boring.
I have zippers that undo me,
and I step from mossy knolls
of magical
to the center of volcanos.
Sometimes I'm a wild flowering currant
and other days,
a simple sloth sipping tea.
Today, however,
I'm embracing
all the edges of me.

You'd be Dead if You Didn't Feel

"I'm falling hard," she blinked before sunrise was awake. The norm of routine caught her as she made breakfast. Sometimes it helps to feed the toaster bread and listen to the stir-click-plop of oatmeal filling a bowl warm. But it wasn't until the hoot of a single owl brought her back to the real feels.

She spoke from the hush of her thoughts, "My days have been full of worry and fear." They hadn't talked in a while, but a slivery-sensing owl was near and didn't spare a beat from its wise-precise-curved-beak.

> *"You'd be dead if you didn't feel. You wouldn't be you if you didn't see the calamity surrounding the fields. You are probably the tenderest soul I've met in my 64 or so years.*
>
> *Why? I won't let you answer because you have this ability to lower your eyes without breathing and somehow disappear. You see-hear-feel others, but when it comes to seeing who you are, you really don't know, do you?*
>
> *So, I will tell you.*
>
> *Let it be known I visit often. I watch for the late-night light to click dim and see you stir before dawn. That's who you are. I sing to let you know, you are never alone. So, write something today. Pretty or not but understand it is okay to cry, rant, scream and throw something hard. Crash the sound barriers and keep touching those full stars. Somehow your aliveness is kin to the angst and joy of those living and gone—it's a soulful art. This is you—inside-full-beautiful. Just as you are."*

HEART-PATH

With a candlelight
of a thousand stars
those who can't see
will reject who you are.

Let them not dismiss
your inner dream-speak;
only you are aware
of the heart-path you seek.

SOUL'S THOUGHTS

Pressing her skin beside a quiet-focus, her meditations could have threaded a needle with the golden wisp of a sprite's laughter. Increments of time stitched lazily and were bathed in hushed concentric circles of drowsy-warm. Just as she was about to open her eyes, a speck appeared; it was about the circumference of a ladybug's dot. Curiously she peeked inside and saw a rare view. It was the glimpse of her inner beauty touching other soul's thoughts.

LOVE WRITES ME

I often awake before sunrise and putter slowly.
I rarely speak human for hours.
Thinking is more in images.
Night dreams surface in silhouetted feels
while I take such pleasure
stirring cream in my coffee.
Mugs are meant to be curled around
and today, seeing a morning moon,
it is extra exquisitely mystical.
My agenda of 'to-do'
remains a lovely-fuzzy list
hosted within a canary lined cage/page or two
(or three…. truthfully more).
But for now,
my fingertips are a direct transfusion
slow dancing from heart.
Something happens here.
I become morning and moon and coffee
and words weep through.
This is sacred.
This quiet is the core of my heart.

I love when
all my feels
are cushioned
in the softest silence
of a sleepy snow.

YOU MATTER

Sometimes, I can't help but think
I am an alien wanting to drink
the shortest strings of poetry.

"You matter.
I believe you.
Hold me.
I love you."

And then I wonder
are there other aliens out there?
Breathing and being weird
and wondering the same thing?

Maybe we'll meet by the sea
and this won't just be a dream.

"You matter.
I believe you.
Hold me.
I love you."

To Be Loved

My wish for you
{{and me}}
is to be loved
so fiercely
it is tender
and true.

To have
such a love
that defends,
is believed in
and treated equally.

To freely cry,
rage and still be
loved in our
unseen shadows.

My wish for you
{{and me}}
is to be loved
with our imperfections
and still be an absolute.

SECTION II

Love Is

Dreams spoke fluently on a tea-stained parchment. I gathered my courage and read my words:

"What love is not, has taught me more about what love is. The charade that love is always perfect, creates an empty-full. For I believe we have feathered souls. The dark and our light bleeds. We equally soar and sink. Love can't be well-defined and that's exquisite; because love is a celebration for us to unfold."

EARTH IS A DANCE

It's beyond me and yet somehow, I know…
When there's a patch in the sky
it turns to a window; I must sundial
its whispers and follow its call.

Like the arm of a rose just knows
thorns protect as petals of heart grow.

Where dreaming knows
earth is a dance
under moonlit trees,
drumming into rivers
beneath what is seen.

It's beyond me and yet somehow, I know…

There's flight in this mysterious magic
to distill just how we find
ethereal links with other souls;

I believe this is love
felt through a sky-window.

WILDEST BLOOMS

Love is like a fruit tree. In winter she's the silent sound of leafless but her inner circles ring. I hear her barren branches bear wild blooms and bees bring nectar to turn her fruit. The seasons unfold her bold. Love grows her heavier and branches bend—it gives and takes us through storm and warms. Love bears us fruit on the shy nigh of our highest form. The gnarled branches transcend what is and isn't. Love's core carries her seeds. It's well planted in the palms of hands and welcomes the ranges of grief and joy to water her land. 'There'—I don't know exactly where but I feel love becomes the sun and moon; the sweetness born of barren branches—aged from her wildest blooms.

DISCOVERY

Let's keep stretching
to find the mosaic
of our truest dreams;
the imperfection
of our perfection
and the discovery
of our unfolding.

LOVE'S JOYS

I am grateful for you and lemon trees.
Blue Clouds dipped in ice-cream.
Friends who transcend
and understand.
Poetry and cinnamon.
Milky moonlit trees.
A particular feline's
purring-fusion.

Love in a sunrise.
Bees buzzing a melody.
Evergreens. Sentient rocks.
Silent shores. Fireplaces warm.
Cookies and morsels of dark chocolate.
Sipping lattes with elephants.
Stirring soul's imagination.
Flannel grey.

Whale's soulful songs.
Naps and dreams.
Music. Stormy seas.
A hummingbird's flight
and nectar's delights.
Small cafés.
Autumn's descent.
Zen's quietness.
Rainy twilight.

Word ponds and serious diving.
Tears spent with those in silence.
I am grateful for
love's joy.

Rose Soaked Rhapsody

Some moments
feel forever familiar
like rain skimmed pines
my heart aware,
quickens my ears
explores my skin
to cathedral wild
I sway absently
forgetting body shy
as if I'm
a rose soaked rhapsody
with a rain filled sky.

Soft, Gentle, Soft

When the winds set the sun down,
I pull the blinds up fuller
to hear twilight cast blinks
over steadfast queries

'Soft
Gentle
Soft'

Whisper the first stars.
Your deepest answers
are in your heart.

THE ART OF TEA

There's something irresistible, how the ritual of making tea—welcomes stillness—as if nothing else matters. Hot water embraces tea leaves as earthenware watches the steam. We blend well. Much like gentleness impresses upon a heart or how midnight's quiet is a modern dance with soul. I feel humble within this soft, safe space of divinity—trusting the peace of here and now. It brings eye-smiles and the sweetest cleansing tears to see clearer for another tomorrow.

I hear music when rain kisses midnight and darkness ushers in the waking of dawn.

HEARTS

The veil,
is joy of light and
wings of solemn sanctuary.

Its flight,
a wisp of soundless threads
and voice of dancing spirits.

A sojourn,
of delicate and earth
hearts parched to understand.

Slate upon sand
sea upon edges
and a depth of tide's knowing.

A walk,
between sheer and listen
the message is,
to love.

SUMMONED BY MOONLIGHT

Breath felt complete
as evening dawns;
a sky mapped
of silvery threads
an intuitive surrender,
she is spirit
as I am
she.

SQUARE ROOT OF NOTHINGNESS

Some days
lend best
with the square root
of nothingness.
Less worry
welcomes warm stills
and words spill.
Love knows and
solitude fills.

A CIRCLE OF HOLY

Nature. Music. Art. Cookies. Nap.
Tea. Walk. Talk. Weep.
Candlelight. Blankets. Compassion.
Words weave shelter.
Love writes.
Read softly. Comfort.
Sing gently. Feel the feels.
Quiet much.
Pianos touch.
Cozy soft socks.
Speak out. Listen full.
Hear clear.
Dream.
This is my circle
of holy.

GRIEF'S LOVE

Grief's love is transparency
the shudder of silent loss
a scrape of thorn against paint
shuttered eyes locked
with pine barren thoughts;
I walk with shadow's trees
shoreline drawn erratic
for grief's love escapes
from lips cracked
of aged memories
and dream, may I,
on a Heron's wingspan
to current safety
nary, nonetheless the whole
essence of grief's love.

Originally published in *Hidden Lights: A Collection of Truths Not Often Told*, 2017.

IMAGINATION

I became the sea
for just a while;
grey and full
sunlight not lit.
Hammered waves
lifted twisted inside cove;
white spray accentuated
my fingertips.
Until I spoke
and the words were feels
solid, strong, sensuous
supplementing a soft, singing real.

LOVE IS

Layers of mittens.
Lamb-soft-socks.
Shoveling a meditation.
Wet boots.
Brushing off branches
held heavy by snowy storm.
Heartfelt whispers.
Tree-speak is warm.
Soup sips and bread dips.
A quiet night with owl song.
Cat nestled. Books shelter.
We perch near a fire warm.

Kindness is the sea speaking and compassion has a quality of endless; a transparency of realness. It feels between a rib's hull and transposes the soul. It sees inside hearts.

TIRED

Words tumbled
over tongue and
script weary.

The sun cried,

"Can you still hear me?"

Walk with me
 along budding greens;
'til the bells of each petal
will wash your tired holy.

DEEPLY FELT

I'm in that eye-closed-place
where I keep hearing small cries
of 'what-about-me?'

The parent. The loner.
The quiet. The homeless.
The single. The divorced.
The friendless. The sick.
The hurting.

Not included in the festivities
of what seems the majority
on a day called holy.

I cry when I hear
those not being seen.
It filters through tree's sap and I

press,
press,
press
my knees way
down,
down,
down.
And pray.

Earth speaks
a handful of indigo stardust;
and oh how, I ask
please send the clouds

to wrap around
so many aching shoulders,
with a
deep,
deep,
deep
felt love.

JONI MITCHELL LIKE

Soft thoughts
between steamed milked sighs.
Laces of espresso spills.
People sights.
Music drifts
Joni Mitchell-like.
Time aged still.
Funny thoughts slip into word smiles
as I write across the miles
to bring a friend near.
Blink-a-bit for throat swallows a tear.
Alone, but not, as soft thoughts
touch my heart in a coffee shop.

Because we need
silence after storms
to see-hear beneath
where raindrops speak
a 1000 tongue
of gentleness.

OUT THERE

His herringbone tweed and patched sleeves filled the space with ease. Rumpled, with wear, his walk spoke effortlessly. Comfortable with the lack of conformity. Ageless with humility. A soft smile centered in his eyes. Words came before speaking and weighted in poignancy. At first glance the room stop. Suspended liquid mercury formed reflective droplets. Just enough time to think and feel through the aggregated textures; spackled walls, Berber carpet, lights set warm. Emotions elevated to sense and feel the caliber of authenticity. Intuition fluttered at speeds unseen. Skin raised to the tempo of the elements. Sounds shifted. And then she knew. Real is real. Her candor would stand solid in her truths. Without underestimating herself she initiated the words hanging intimately and introduced herself.

Late afternoon
is a cup full of pages
curling around thoughts
fading easily into a daydream.

Colors Under My Skin

I hear colors of late sun bobbing under my skin; leaves paint clouds and vines dot an outline of braille. For nothing in this moment is ordinary. Moss could be a tree. Rivers could be heaven. Rain drizzles freely like pebbles skimming seas. Sometimes it's okay to not be quite sure. Otherwise, how would one hear colors and breathe through eyes that once could see? How would I have known, that the dot of vines was only pointing at my heart to find me?

CIRCLES

I searched for words
to release circles of
peaceful
gentle
love
nothing came until
a candle's flame eclipsed
a soaring dove.
And in that instance
Forever was the circle of all.

WHAT IS LOVE?

The silence of early awake. Music's soul-speak. Humility embracing kindness. Seeing quiet. Tears expressing dreams. Love blinked from eyelashes. Warmth of a hug. Space forever in time. The pause after I-love-you is full and felt. The inhale of hope and the exhale of peace. Soft grey with ocean spray. A mountain's crescendo. Rivers singing a lament. Despair is the living in dying. Favorite books comfort. Alone isn't always lonely. A cradled mug of stars and thoughts. Touch can be holy. Footsteps that bring tea. Clear birdsongs felt before sung. The turn of key, voices safety. A shelter of earned trust. Words not bent when shared. Breathing with heartbeat.

Writing this is a soulful prayer.

JOYING IS LIVING

Last night the sky must have been dancing
because when I awoke stardust
was clinging to each frosty shade of wintering.
I heard angelic singing and ringing
of sun soaked tiny bells gleaming.
I might have cried a bit too
for joying is living
in the simplicity of seeing
that loving is aching
as it is in rejoicing.

WHEN LOVE IS REAL

Small things, like a note with meaning, a hug with feel, love's consistency and commitment have the tenacity of real. I hold those things freely and sacredly because they are precious. We learn to trust as the vessel of all relationships expand and grow. The vicious tides will surface too and there will always be disappointments, chaos or incongruent feels. Nevertheless, the storms unearth a clearer soul; the eyes of hearing through the dissonance leads us to a warm place where kindness rules.

The earth
is weeping
the Blues,
against a
satin grey sky
Love.
Be love.
Feel love.
Nature is love.

Silence Becomes the Words

Some mornings, when the stillness is seeable, and the air has fringes of birdsong, I can lay on the lips of listening and hear the space between nature's thoughts.

That silent sigh of a head nod, the tone of body sway, that eye flicker of irresistible joy-speak. The chalice where kindness knows how edges break and without fixing—pauses to let the moment breathe. Silence becomes the words.

I'm reminded how it is a fierce respect of growing trust as boundaries follow a *rivered* well of depth. It is very much like, music—it has a language that reverberates what rises in heart. It is felt under skin, to union with marrow of all senses.

This is the intelligence of soul to soul. It becomes the ability to walk with empathy and to feel everything and to somehow know: We are a mosaic masterpiece of love.

OUR DREAMING SONG

Walk with me,
as we watch the blinks of a half-moon.
Something primal and sacred
in the tone of simple. A grace
and reverence with dark fluted blues;
it's endless really—a seamless portal
of what will be
and is and felt
in a slight hum.
It's our dreaming song.

THANKING LOVE

I slipped outside
to thank the stars,
welcome the moon
and hear between
the thickets.

Oh, those trees adore
the wash of moonlight.
Their voices amplified
and I was lifted. This sound
can soothe the tenor of souls.

Together we shared
a tiny patch and witnessed
the wisdom of a billion years,
suspended above,
as a luminescent pearl
radiating love.

Go slowly.
Go softly.
Rest.
Still.
Take to what is holy;
and feel
how infinity connects
you and me.

Love is felt
at the corner
of music
and raindrops.

L–O–V–E

Spell me love
without the letters.
Show me the same feels
as rain befalls sodden flowers.
Feel me as breath rises with sun
and knows the heart of a circle.
Flow with me like the moon
promises the sea,
a daily kiss beside shore.
Spell me love
as a companion
weathered in respect;
created as a symbiosis of real.
And I will know
this love is pure.

Love often slips from my eye's soul.

BEING LOVED

I never knew
how tender-sad
it would be
to witness
what love is.

With each tear
another star filled
the owl-sung night.

The fullness of Moon
gently nodded,

"What you are feeling
is the dreaming of you
being loved too.
I know this to be true;
I've been watching you
for a very, very long time."

HOME

I had other words, late, late, last night but they drifted between the pillow and the moon. I hung them on a ledge, to keep safe, until I could find the space and rhythm for them to speak true.

Saucers of honey spilled from the heavens and waves upon waves of solace raised me to see the vestige of quiet's vast balm. It was a poetic sight of birds in flight through the deep sky's blues.

I counted love's ache in the heartbeat of a metronome and a song played along. We became a duet with skin as if one with the sea. Clouds harmonized and there was a distinct hum of fairies.

I believe when we are feeling that deeply—to the inside and vibration of bone—there's an invisible source of something. Let's call it soul. That very place where darkness is as much as light and the ground is hard and yet soft; it welcomes us home.

Relationships
What Love is and isn't

This is love in action.
It's not always the high-highs
but the real-reals.
The day-to-day nomenclature
of companionship.
It's the center of empathy.
And the translation of
something we often can't physically see
but there's an unspoken essence
of shared vulnerability.
That very touching expression
—is love.

GOODBYES HAVE FULL MEMORIES

I keep getting glimpses of
beach bone sand walls
and rock quarried deep-seated ledges.
Time ticks to keystrokes
and pages turn to wind-spoken words.

I keep hearing seasons spin
as something nudges me closer,
almost eagerly
like a prepubescent dawn;
naïvely, it underlays my skin,
outwardly, though
I have grown distinct lined ridges.

I push my newish bluish readers
a little less south. Vertical, Northwest lines
accentuate the earned map of my forehead
and my eyes tell stories
I have yet to transpose.

I feel the sun rise
through moss-heavy cedar fences
there I hold;
I hold onto the warmth
of a blanketed dark roast and
saline rushes in unexpectedly;
for goodbyes are eminent
as much as hellos
except goodbyes
have fuller memories.

LETTING GO

I see love's art play
sprayed on concrete walls.
Graffiti claims boldly
love isn't always real
when it speaks in double time.
Hurt hidden in minor chords
a heartache out of reach;
but you don't know.

I hear it though
and it will be okay
because of this,
I'm told.
I'll be stronger and how
my time isn't now.
While a pillar of seasons
stands between us.
So, I'll shed me wild and
let go of what isn't.

LET'S BE FLIGHT'S LOVE

For just a few…
let's breathe
and touch wordless cool
through similar strains of
hands bowed
dropping our guard
fears softened tender
seeing how vulnerable
creates a shadow of courage
let's respect
swollen
vented
hurts
just for a few…
let's be
flight's love.

WHAT ISN'T SAID

There's often depth to what isn't said. That side glance, furrowed brow, the tentative pause, the lingering and holding of a sentence. Each word takes on a vibration until just the right sound variation rises or falls from somewhere like sea mist and grey filaments of fog or the base of a fallen tree and how lichen knows to cling; it's a symbiotic relationship of contrast and similar and being. Maybe it's also the stillness that captivates me. A titration and feel into the polarity of fields like the crest before a wave touches shore and the timbre of clarity in winter's first snowfall. How summer's humidity dampens my thoughts. I'm pulled to the center of nothing and wrapped pure by it all.

TO LOVE AGAIN

I could say
I will not let
anyone
hurt me
ever again.
Nor let love
lilt upon heart.

Yet I know
this isn't true.
For I've tried
and learned.

Love hurts.
It also breathes
and stretches;
it offers inexplicable
changes
with or without
the conflux of
agreement.

Love in all forms
is capable
of stirring infinity.
We gain and lose
and still
I will always
choose
to love again.

RESPECT

The essence of relationships is a mixture of respect, love and consistency. It's not linear and at times miscommunication or differences can challenge. However, the effort to make things work can't be one-sided otherwise there's an imbalance. We don't grow when people in our lives reject, ignore and dismiss who we are. Self-respect teaches us there's freedom when we let go of those who diminish our spirit, repress our dreams and control us. So, from experience, I trust those who show me by their actions. Such people are caring, multi-dimensional, diverse, giving and respecting. They believe, support and respect individual growth.

Friendship

How is it that we meet? I believe this is part of the chemistry in our soul's soup. We react when the alchemy is ready. These complex and daring relationships embody a transparence that allows the expansion of our individual growth plates. We strengthen, bend, and stretch because we are encouraged to grow.

You Didn't Notice

Maybe you didn't hear me because the dryer was moaning, and the dishes had piled up to the sky. I might have dropped a few to see if you noticed but maybe you didn't hear me over the baby's cry.

I thought more than once, wouldn't it be easy to walk out that door and just keep walking and walking but maybe you didn't hear me because I closed the bedroom door so softly; I didn't want to disturb your snore and then fear your roar. I could only rock one child at a time to keep things on the quiet side.

Maybe you didn't notice me because I could disappear even when you were near. Sometimes I wished I were invisible but maybe I did it too well and I was. A smile can hide but eyes can't lie; they see the maybes and *shoulds* and *coulds* and wishes all held closely; because maybe I was the only one who could hear me crying inside.

WHOLENESS NEEDS SUPPORT

If I ask you, please listen. I'm cautiously weighing the feelings that tremble over nefarious waves. Am I worthy to pursue the unwritten script of this living?

Open please to tender heart and hear me say, over brunt, bruised bones, misgivings can confuse. Archives of silenced anger can be displaced. Feelings isolated to lesser or more, calls in shame.

Let those voices be heard.

Separating self from what was and what is, asks heavily to lean on comfort of earth. Nature knows. Go gentle, is voiced on frosted gate; she paints shadows of decay and rebirth.

Walk with me, silently, as the water rises and aches; sea storm stories sometimes roar before they soar. It is not because I'm needy or in want for more.

I'm integrating. Wholeness needs support.

Letting Go, Isn't Easy

The beginning,
I remember well,
the countless hours
weaved with tiny hands.
I wore layered beads
of endearments.

My breath
birthed new ones with ease
sugared snapped sweetness
mocha munchkins
baby squirrel
sort of surprised they
weren't confused
but love laced my words.

I remember well
the long feverish nights
crying skinned knees
kisses of stinky toes
band aides to ease
warm baths to soothe
sleepless in the ICU
swallowing my tears
holding them dear
while tiny socks

grew
and
grew
But now?
Please stop
reminding me

what was and
what isn't...
I know and see
the fun you send
across Wi-Fi's high
of *snapchating* and
texting the waves of
WhatsApping
I remember well
without
you.

STAINED-GLASS WINGS

What if we learn to flow with life's river and let us be drenched with the axil of earth's ministering and united with the eclipse of our gifts? Where we surf the textures through forested degrees of our being, as skyscrapers and people met us as gratefully as trees feed us. Somehow knowing this is real: to stretch completely until our shadows are as visible as our quirks are real.

To me, this is the unfolding of our stained-glass wings; the very ones that heighten as we soar with bass to treble notes reveal us.

BOUNDARIES

When I need a reminder...
of who and what is real and true
away from deadly spaces
where our soul
can get battered and bruised
boundaries can be tested,
twisted and confused
kindness needs to know
it is not a weakness
and maybe,
betrayal is a siren's cry to
knit a safety net around heart
this is when I know...
I must fold into my garden
where nature is always real
and kindness does matter
and love will find the truth.

Nothing is Forever

There are rare relationships—pure exceptions—that weave wisps of night-ebony, whale-grey, and heart-blue into our lives. We trust them, and they trust us. The feral blocks of self-preservation dissipate and there's an open field, wide mountains, endless seas, gifting us to navigate this human world of connections, with such relationships and dreams.

Ordinary is Extraordinary

Whiplashed heart
crushed to bare glass blue
weary to bone's core.
Keystrokes still fused
with virtual inkblot stares;
surreal, is the feel
of feathery parchment.
She crafts it to safe sailboat size
and voyages inner tempest
of why; and sees ordinary people
share their extraordinary stories
and cries deep sea blue.

I Am Not You

I tried to be
what you wanted.
I tried to be different.
I pretended to be
who I wasn't.

Time and time again
I fought
against my real.

Until I spun
myself inward
only to see,
I am freedom's fringe.

I am not you
nor you me
and the path I take
is not glam or glitzy
it is soft and often lonely.

Sometimes I cry
as you walk by;
you can't see me
for I am different.

I quiver with ecstasy
of wind inspired daydreams
and plunge to the land somber;

I tried for so long
to fit in

only to find my quiet
sees authenticity.
I don't want
to follow what isn't me
I hear angels speak
and dancing drums beat
It is more than okay
to be me.

No Longer Chasing You

I will no longer chase the ghost of you. The flare of your fine shines and cuts blind. The click of your shoes. The tuck of classic. My tongue tastes powdered plastic. I've grown weaker watching you toss small hard biscuits of binary sharp platitudes. Cursory words hurt. I admit, my fragile hope wanted to hear us think in the art of share and speak. Yet you said "no" in a dozen polite circles of dizzy elite. I will no longer chase the ghost of you. For in my quiet, I am more complete without you.

There is a universal language of love which is real, and it is spoken in a thousand ways to teach us about each other and our truths.

UNSPOKEN

Our body language
is an intriguing dance
of the unspoken.
When it oxidizes
into the channels
of our perceptive ability
it gives more meaning
than most words.

You

I saw your shy-soft smile
curve 'round riverbed
teeming full
with swelling
prose of living.

I felt your thoughts
streaming
understated and
yet transforming into
something beautiful.

JUST A LIFETIME

I'm almost there
where I could
hold your hand
and squeeze raw
sentences unfiltered
into the palm of nature.

I'm almost knowing
how complex is creative
and how shattered
isn't empty but
pieces rearranged
from origin nullified.

I'm almost accepting
this soul-body
as brushstrokes of
salted sea-clouds;
where stillness is
the cadence and
quiet matters.

And I am
fully believing
this kaleidoscope of living
will take a lifespan
of transcending
the rapids of unfolding
my heart's seasons rhythm.

No Perfect Needed

You didn't have to say much
because I could feel
the nod-pause of your seeing.
I shared, and you believed.
No perfect needed.
My feathers once scattered
soon became wings.
So simple sounding
yet being heard is sacred.
Something gentle happens.
It's mystical.
A welcoming loop
is created in a symbiosis
to translate
a newly born set
of hieroglyphs.
The center is love.

WORDS CAN BITE

You seemed real and kind
like honey sliced fruit
but truly there's less
and less there. Actions
speak. Words are biting;
supporting only
a god given few.

To say
I don't feel
excluded
would be a lie.

I do.

It hurts.
I cry inside.
I challenge and,
I'm chastised.
Tables turned lopsided
and I'm the one shamed.

Therefore, I must
protect myself.
Pulling far from such
fated-fake. I'll swim with a pod of
whales, gathered off-shore;
deeper bonds are those who can soar.

JUST A NOTE

Please read this note
crumbled again, and again
because I've written it
a dozen times
and I'm uneasy to say
it holds the sounds of green
and feels heavy from rain;
the sea has swallowed
me whole.

Please press it flat
and read each word.
Not a cursory glance
of 'that's nice' and
'wow, it's fine'.
I know empty. It rattles shallow
against beaten shadows.
Stops me cold each time.

Please know this note
holds more than words
but hears candlelight
and voices of dark wine.

Please close your eyes
to the pulse of rain
as it soothes wild canvas
of green; and
knows a lifetime of messages
are written between
the lines of this crumbled note.

PAIN

I won't keep explaining why
aggression causes pain
the double knotted
twisted words
the shame
knife jabbing
to slash me empty
when below the channels
Your only gain is to hurt me.

TONGUE-TIED

I can't remember
the last time you said
something kind
without cords
heavy and convoluted
leaving me tongue-tied
and heart-spent.
I'd speak too soon
to fill the thought-gaps
settling, dust-like
but now and here
grateful the glare
of shadow's light
lets me see
what isn't
and is true.

Because of You

You didn't have to speak.
I felt a transcendence of
two hearts beat.

An inner sanctum for souls
hands-holding stillness,
an indelible love-respect-whole
drifting on edges anew;
circles kept overlapping.

You didn't have
to speak. I already knew
our paths crossed and I
would never have you.

Then I understood
I'm the sunrise at sea,
the lighthouse at dusk
seeking someone like you.

Shades of soft sounds rose
all around. Because of you
I can see me; I'm worth more
than I ever knew.

You frightened me
because I started
to feel
a swell
of how
love is real.

JUST DANCE

What say you,
on this summer night when
bees begin heart-buzz at dawn?

All I can do is embrace your surreal;
sun's setting has got me all hypnotic.

Surely, you too can hear stained-glass leaves
quiver. It's okay to say yes. For I can
taste the shiver in you.

Some connections stretch
on the warble of what we see-feel;
it's enraptured by lavender's feathered Blues.

The swell of this magic repeats
a blushed infusion;
night rises with crescent.

What say you,
if we could just dance
in tonight's moonlight?
And let the trees be
the soft silent of our kindness.

By the River

Meet me by the river
and I'll share a story
about the crow who sang
to the setting sun.

I'll take a stick
and sketch images
and paint a field of wild
and wonder and mysterious.

Petals will unfold like fingers
touching the very notes
of scarlet faded skies.

Meet me by the river
and we'll watch the sun drink
and fill the moon with hope;
and raise a nightlight in the sky.

The threshold
of my boundaries
has been violated.
And my soul
is bruised.

I Tried

I could have settled
and I did try
to tuck and fold,
our towels
hung side by side.

I tried to fit in
but trees don't want ceilings
and clouds breathe seasons;
my heart doesn't do
freeze dry.

I'm wind planted; stormy
at times and calmed by
Nature's lullaby. I straddle
this world and somewhere
far off; where conversations
dive through soul's pooled eyes
and wander over saucers of
ridiculous.

I tried. I really did.
But I almost died. Normal
isn't all that it is. That's why
I had to say goodbye.

PUSH-PULL ME WRONG

I can't begin to tell you
all the reasons why
you push-pull me wrong;
so, I wrote a prayer
and it became a song
and a thousand feathered
percussions strummed a lullaby
because my heart can't beat
on the outside.
So, I wrote a prayer
and it became a song.
Music fills the gaps when
You ignored my love.

I NOTICED

You cut me out.
Set me aside,
as one of those,
who's not good enough.
I wish you knew
how long it took
to be seen by you
only to understand
your judgement shows
how little you know.
Who I am.

I noticed.

THANK YOU

Did you not know
that I depended
upon you so?
Foolish me
for giving you
that control.
When all the while
what I didn't see
was how the power
was already within me.

{{Thank you.}}

Now I'm able to let you go.

Stop It

If I share with you
where sherbet draws
the calls of pre-morning stalls,
it's because I trust you.
I linger there and stir my thoughts
tears may rise and fall.

Don't slam me against
my own dark walls
in those bereft moments of tender.
Arrogance's advice,
is the tutelage of superior,
exposing the flaws of one's interior.

STOP IT.

I'll tell you why.
I can no longer abide
by those who defy my cries.
My daisy-chains have soliloquies;
parchment greys tied
to long-lost days, hostage in closets
so afraid, chasing clover
to find good-luck in a sea of mistrust.

YOU.

My dear (NOT), have threaded one too many
needles over my patchwork quilt;
and so, on this day
watching the sky explain

I KNOW.

You never deserved my love.

LAST POEM I WROTE FOR YOU

I remember the last poem recited;
it was while sipping champagne
and watching the sun,
dissolving over the sea.

I lit a candle
it's what I still do
when spirits of life and
death call me.

I gifted those words
hand over heart
tumbling from a cadence of trust
in the quiet, long after dusk.

The sun found the moon
and my words, strung upon air;
virgin lyrics, spilling from
heart to mouth;
raw, real and tender.

Just shy of the third line
you walked away,
laughing and mocking;
I stopped then sharing
what had come
from inside of me.

SPEAK REAL

When the clover is tired
and the drip, drip, drip
of a gutter reminds you of
all that needs fixing and
there really isn't an end
because
way, way down
in the crawl space
there's a small mousey
(at least it isn't in the housey)
but then life makes you sad;
so, you start thinking
if only more people
could speak real...

You hurt me.
I'm sorry.
I love you.

Then the drip, drip, drip
would become a tambourine
and the clover would be in
a meadow feeding
a hundred goats; the roofer
would be a fiddler and singing
and most definitely the mousey
would be far away under
some warm hay and by then
things would be okay....
because love has a way
of easing those hurting.

Again

You missed the point

again

when my courage was high
but you didn't see
how much it meant
so, you pushed me aside
as if I were a plastic spoon;
but I'll let you know

again

I'm not another letter
drowning in alphabet soup.
I've made a raft
out of oyster crackers
and stitched a sail
embroidered with a promise
to me
not to ask you

again

when something means
so very much
to me.

INSIGHTS

There's a knowing in our deepest of heart. A place of reaching and stretching freely. Where love doesn't burn but warms. It's a place where we can safely see how relationships expand and contract. We exchange places and sail a few experiences in each other's voyage. Misunderstandings can lead to un-relinquished new levels of richness—or not. It hurts. It lifts. We fail. We feel. We try again. We briefly see what we thought we knew. Insights have this uncanny way of tilting and shifting our perspectives. It is here we heal and more than survive we flourish. We learn to navigate compassion's inner opal curve to see the complexities of your eyes thru mine. We surface and wipe the oceans of old and new saline knowing love doesn't always have to burn.

FOR WHAT ISN'T

You misread me
when the sun was blazing
and the heart of my moon
was eclipsed.

You didn't see
the gold in the darkness.
Shadow-speak
is hidden bliss.

I gave. You wanted. I held.
You asked for more than I could be.
I'm no longer seeking
for what isn't.

Those voices I sing
are the soul of my belly.
And the heart of my song
is a love I give freely.

LOVE IS NEVER FAR

My eyelashes are no wider
than tonight's swath
of moon's light;
so I must whisper this
for I fear I'll wake the stars.
Night has consumed me
into liquid pools of mercury.
And yet I still hear an echo...
love
love
love
is never far.

Love me whole
or leave me.
There is no room left
to be abused.

Sit with Me

Just sit with me
on the edge of always
and I'll tell you a story
of how shooting stars
are really angels
and how much
a tangle of wet grass
are lovers holding raindrops.

Just sit with me and
I'll let you trace your fingers
over an imaginative odyssey,
tasting each page as it turns.

Just sit with me all seed-like,
nested in safe shelter
within midnight's
gorgeous brown earth
before thoughts reach
a glade of sun's light.

Just sit with me
in a patch way over there
by sea, or boulder,
or on an edge of a pier
with feet swaying
to the waves of
dreams and tears.
I'll be there.
Sitting and wondering and being
the sky's deep blue with you.

PARCHMENT OF OUR SOUL

Love is the parchment of the soul.
Poetic ink flowers a narrative
with beginnings, middles and ends.

Love can hurt when it is exclusive.
But, I believe, it can flourish when inclusive.
That's when I hear
oceans and ebony see her depths.
Sadness can be there too
hand-in-hand with acceptance.

Love smiles, tears, and conflicts;
it spells genuine. Love is also
frayed, tender, and fragile
and yet each

Letter
Opens
Venues of
Endless
Sentiments.

Love finishes sentences
without a word spoken or many.
Love is rain on evergreens
and restless pillows.
Love is free to say, 'no'.
Love respects.

Love is music on repeat.
Love is an espresso sipped,
hearing stories along cobblestones.
Love grieves. Love is justice.

Love is aged, young, and honeyed,
innocent and wise as it grows.

We need more Love to be written,
read and heard
on the parchment of our souls.

WHEN WE MEET

We haven't met yet
but I know you are out there
by the way the sun kisses my hair
and how love turns silver
when age fills the air. I know
we haven't met yet but I still
feel wisps of eye-smiles skipping along
wordless cobblestones as we watch
shooting stars over the Seine. My mug
sitting next to yours as you tease
at my dreaminess and we sip ideas
with such ease as if we always knew
we were meant to be.

Understand I will quietly slip away from the noisy crowd when I see the pale stars rising, blooming over the oaks. I'll pursue the solitary pathways of the twilight meadows with only this one dream. You come too.

—Rainer Maria Rilke

ABOUT THE AUTHOR

CAROLYN RIKER is a highly sensitive poetic person. She has a private practice as a licensed mental health counselor and teaches. Her first book of poetry and prose, *Blue Clouds* was published in 2016. Followed by an anthology, *Hidden Lights* which she co-edited and contributed to in 2017. She has been published in five anthologies and was a steady columnist for several online journals. *This is Love* is her second collection of poems and poetry. Carolyn enjoys quiet, nature, friends, music and finds joy in small things; dark chocolate knows her well and lattes are a comfort. Her favorite feline is a large ginger who is also a writer and has thoughts about writing children's books.

You can connect with Carolyn at www.carolynriker.com.

Made in the USA
San Bernardino, CA
26 August 2018